W0113792

better together*

* This book is best read together, grownup and kid.

 **akidsco.com**

a kids book about

PRIDE

by Kendall Clawson

A Kids Co.
Editor Emma Wolf
Designer Rick DeLucco
Creative Director Rick DeLucco
Studio Manager Kenya Feldes
Sales Director Melanie Wilkins
Head of Books Jennifer Goldstein
CEO and Founder Jelani Memory

DK
Delhi Technical Team Bimlesh Tiwary Pushpak Tyagi, Rakesh Kumar
Senior Production Editor Jennifer Murray
Senior Production Controller Louise Minihane
Senior Acquisitions Editor Katy Flint
Acquisitions Project Editor Sara Forster
Managing Art Editor Vicky Short
Managing Director, Licensing Mark Searle

First American edition, 2025
Published in the United States by DK Publishing, 1745 Broadway, 20th Floor,
New York, NY 10019

First published in Great Britain in 2025 by
Dorling Kindersley Limited, 20 Vauxhall Bridge Road, London SW1V 2SA
A Penguin Random House Company

The authorised representative in the EEA is
Dorling Kindersley Verlag GmbH. Arnulfstr. 124, 80636 Munich, Germany

Copyright © 2025 Dorling Kindersley Limited
A Kids Book About, Kids Are Ready, and the colophon 'a' are trademarks of A Kids Book About, Inc.
10 9 8 7 6 5 4 3 2
002-349892-April/2025
All rights reserved.
No part of this publication may be reproduced, stored in or introduced into a retrieval system,
or transmitted, in any form, or by any means (electronic, mechanical, photocopying, recording,
or otherwise), without the prior written permission of the copyright owner.

A catalog record for this book is available from the Library of Congress.
A CIP catalogue record for this book is available from the British Library.
ISBN: 978-0-2417-4350-8

DK books are available at special discounts when purchased in bulk for sales
promotions, premiums, fund-raising, or education use. For details, contact:
DK Publishing Special Markets, 1745 Broadway, 20th Floor, New York, NY 10019
SpecialSales@dk.com

Printed and bound in China
www.dk.com
akidsco.com

MIX
Paper | Supporting
responsible forestry
FSC™ C018179

This book was made with Forest
Stewardship Council™ certified
paper – one small step in DK's
commitment to a sustainable future.
**Learn more at www.dk.com/uk/
information/sustainability**

This book is dedicated to all
the LGBTQIA+ heroes who have bravely
fought for the rights of our community, and
to the people who have always helped my inner
light shine the brightest: my parents, Charles
and Annie Clawson, and my wife, Michele.

Intro
for grownups

Pride. How do we talk about something that has become a festive celebration but commemorates decades of protests for human rights? Talking about Pride can get muddled with our views and acceptance of people whose sexual orientation and/or gender identity may differ from our own. And sometimes, those views can minimize what Pride is really about.

People might think Pride is just about parades, costumes, and rainbow flags, but at its core, Pride is new for each generation. Until about a decade ago, it was primarily a protest for equal rights. Today, it celebrates the vibrant and diverse LGBTQIA+ community. Pride continues as a demand to set discrimination aside and celebrate acceptance and freedom to be ourselves without fear.

In addition to a bit of history about Pride as a movement, this book is centered on the joy of having pride—no matter who you are, how you identify, or who you love.

Together, let's celebrate Pride all year long.

My name is
Kendall Clawson.

I live in the Pacific Northwest of the United States.

I am married and have a dog named Blazer.

I love the ocean, traveling the world, and making lamps out of unexpected things.

I am a member of the LGBTQIA+ community.

Here's a little bit about what those letters mean when people use them to identify* themselves:

*The meaning of these words have changed a lot over the years and will continue to change with each generation.

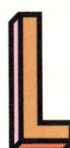 - lesbian (a woman who is primarily attracted to other women)

 - gay (a man who is primarily attracted to other men)

 - bisexual (a person who is attracted to both men and women)

 - transgender (a person whose gender identity differs from their gender assigned at birth)

 - questioning (a person who is exploring who they are attracted to) or queer [the LGBTQIA+ community and people with fluid, shifting identities]

 - intersex (a person who was born with traits that are not exclusively male or female)

 - asexual (a person who doesn't experience attraction to anyone)

 The plus sign is for all the other ways people express themselves as well as for LGBTQIA+ allies, who stand up for, support, and encourage members of this community.

Now that you know who we are, let's talk

about why I wrote this book—it's all about

Everyone wants to be accepted for who they really are.

Think about it like this:

Every person has a light inside of them, which represents everything that makes them unique.

(It's important you know I'm not talking about a lightbulb or a flashlight! This light is your spirit, that special thing inside of you that makes you, YOU.)

When you feel pride, your light shines so brightly that other people can see and feel it.

But when someone feels misunderstood or unable to be themselves, that light has a really hard time coming through.

Pride today is about encouraging everyone to shine as bright as can be, honoring AND celebrating what makes each of us special.

WHY DO WE CELEBRATE?

Well, for as long as
there have been people,
LGBTQIA+ people
have existed.

And many have been discriminated against because of who they love, even to the point of being kicked out of their families, jailed, considered mentally ill, or killed.

This community has been fighting against discrimination and demanding freedom to be themselves since... well, a really long time.

But on June 28, 1969,
the demand for freedom
was so great it could
not be ignored.

It all started at a place
called the Stonewall Inn
in New York City.

The Stonewall Inn
was a place where
members of the LGBTQIA+
community gathered
(and still do today).

They listened to music.

And danced.

And made friends.

And built community.

And felt accepted.

Why was this so important?

Because back then it was considered wrong, and even illegal, for members of the LGBTQIA+ community to do everyday things like:

 hold hands in public with their partners,

 get married,

 have a family,

 visit their partners in the hospital,

 find jobs,

 travel safely,

 wear clothes that reflected their true gender identity,

 or even just spend time together in groups.

One day, at the Stonewall Inn, the police showed up while people were hanging out.

Tired of being harassed, the people stood their ground and demanded peace.

The police started to beat them up and arrest them.

A group of transgender women decided they didn't want to take it anymore.

SO THEY
GHT
BACK.

And more people came
to support them. And even *more*
people came after that.

This was the moment the **entire** LGBTQIA+ community said,

"We're not going to take this anymore."

They were tired of being beaten down, so they rose up against the people who hurt them.

So, every June, we honor that historical moment and celebrate the pride we have in being ourselves and letting our inner lights shine brightly.

How do we celebrate?

We throw a huge party!

We have parades.

We wear bright colors and glitter.

We fly rainbow-colored flags with colors that represent all of the members of our diverse community.

That day at Stonewall was an important moment in our history because it inspired people to protest together, work for recognition and protection, create change, and build community.

People like...

MARSHA P. JOHNSON

and

SYLVIA RIVERA,

transgender women who were leaders in the Stonewall Uprising.

BAYARD RUSTIN,

a gay man who organized the March on Washington* with Dr. Martin Luther King Jr.

*The March on Washington was a huge march in Washington, DC, to demand civil rights for Black people.

HARVEY MILK,

the first openly gay
elected public official.

AUDRE LORDE,

a Black lesbian who wrote books, articles, and poems to protest racism, sexism,* and homophobia.*

*Sexism is the discrimination against someone on the basis of their sex.
*Homophobia is prejudice against homosexual people.

JEANNE MANFORD,

the mom of a gay son,
who started PFLAG (Parents,
Family, and Friends of Lesbians
and Gays), an organization
that supports grownups
with LGBTQIA+ kids.

So there are a lot of big ways
and big reasons we celebrate Pride.

However, celebrating Pride
doesn't end in June.

We can celebrate
Pride all year long.

How?

By standing up for others.

By inviting other people
into your community.

And by believing in yourself,
even when it seems like
no one else does.

What makes you feel pride?

Tell your grownup a few things about yourself that you're proud of.

Ask your grownup to tell you what makes them proud of themselves and proud of you too.

I know each of us is stronger
when we feel proud of the things
we do and how we show up
for other people.

I also know all people need
a space that feels safe to be
just who they are.

That's why we create communities to celebrate Pride and celebrate one another.

When you have pride,

ANYT

HING
IS POSSIBLE.

And when all of us have pride,

THING
IS POSSIBLE.

Each generation has heroes who build on what those before them have created.

Being a hero means using your voice and standing up for what you believe.

Maybe you are that person
for your generation.

HOW BRIGHT WILL YOUR LIGHT SHINE?

Outro
for grownups

Hey there! Now that you have finished this book about Pride, I hope you will celebrate all year long. As you continue talking about the meaning of Pride, I invite you to try out a few things to keep that feeling of Pride going.

1. Tell each other, frequently, what makes you feel pride. Did you show kindness to someone today? Did you stand up for yourself or a friend? Saying what makes you feel pride keeps that feeling alive!

2. Remind yourselves about Pride with an art project. Whether it's making rainbows, or drawing a picture of the light shining inside you, use art as a way to keep the spirit of Pride strong no matter what time of the year it is!

3. Join in the Pride celebration. If there is a Pride parade or a special Pride event in your community, gather your friends and family and join in the fun. Pride is filled with lots of folks who would love to see you there! And don't forget to tell them, "Happy Pride!"

About The Author

Kendall Clawson (she/her) learned to believe in herself from her mother, Annie, who was an elementary school teacher. Every year, parents would angle to get their 3rd graders into her class because she always taught with clarity and love. She ensured her students learned their numbers and letters, and that they also knew they were good people with gifts to share, if they believed in themselves.

Kendall wrote this book while her mother fought her battle with Parkinson's Disease. Every word is a reminder of the importance in lifting up the people we love.

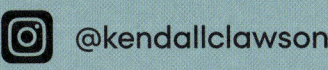 @kendallclawson 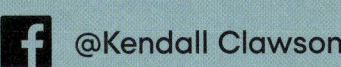 @Kendall Clawson

Made to empower.

a kids book about **racism**
by Jelani Memory

a kids book about ANXIETY
by Ross Szabo

a kids book about DISABILITY
by Kristine Napper

a kids book about IMAGINATION
by LEVAR BURTON

a kids book about belonging
by Kevin Carroll

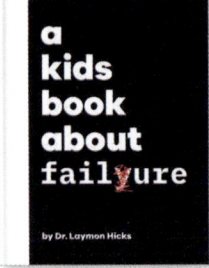
a kids book about failure
by Dr. Laymon Hicks

a kids book about GRATITUDE
by Ben Kenyon

a kids book about LIFE ONLINE
by Dave S. Anderson & Blake Fleischacker

a kids book about body image
by Rebecca Alexander

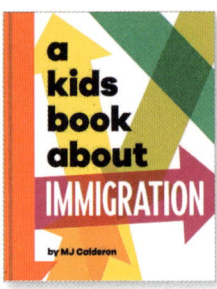
a kids book about IMMIGRATION
by MJ Calderon

a kids book about EMPATHY
by Daron K. Roberts

a kids book about GENDER
by Dale Mueller

a kids book about Love
by ZIGGY MARLEY

a kids book about EQUALITY
by BILLIE JEAN KING

a kids book about MONEY
by Adam Stramwasser

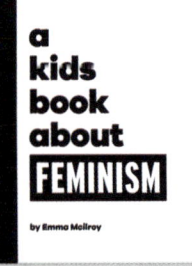
a kids book about FEMINISM
by Emma Mcilroy

a kids book about adventure
by Dr. Ben Tertin

a kids book about CLIMATE CHANGE
by Zanagee Artis & Olivia Greenspan

a kids book about CONFIDENCE
by Joy Cho

a kids book about BEING NONBINARY
by Hunter Chinn-Raicht
in partnership with The GenderCool Project

Discover more at akidsco.com